Egon Schiele

Pomegranate Artbooks ❧ San Francisco

A Book of Postcards

Pomegranate Artbooks
Box 6099
Rohnert Park, CA 94927

ISBN 1-56640-963-2
Pomegranate Catalog No. A709

Pomegranate publishes
books of postcards
on a wide range of subjects.
Please write to the publisher
for more information.

The short span of Egon Schiele's life (1890–1918) is disproportionate to his accomplishments as an artist. Active in Vienna for only eight years, Schiele produced a body of work that, in its abandonment of formal and decorative values, set the stage for Expressionism. His career, however, was nothing short of a constant war with the Establishment and the authorities; the overtly erotic content of much of his work, stark and without embellishment, made him a target of the old order. In the end, Schiele's paintings and drawings can be seen as a parallel development to the fall of the Austro-Hungarian Empire.

Much has been written about Schiele's life and art. To many, the two seem intertwined to the point of being indiscernible. Much of his work is unsettling—even shocking—reflecting a psychological intensity and a propensity for self-exploration and exposure of the vulnerabilities observed in his subjects. His preoccupation with exploring the baser sides of himself and his subjects resulted in an oeuvre that is complex, if not sensitive or sublime. It has been said that Schiele could not pass a mirror without stopping to study his reflection for an extended period. Indeed, in many of his paintings, the mirror either plays a minor role or is a major focus. Schiele observed himself and the world in which he lived with unabashed honesty, holding up a mirror both to himself and to his society.

Egon Schiele applied to the Academy of Fine Arts in Vienna in 1906. There he received his academic training and made the acquaintance of several Jugendstil artists, including Gustav Klimt, who would have a marked influence on him. Schiele first exhibited at Klosterneuberg in 1908 and the following year was represented by four pieces in the international Vienna Kunstschau. In the spring of 1909, dissatisfied with the curriculum, he left the Academy and with several friends started the Neukunstgruppe. That same year also marked his association with the Wiener Werkstätte. By 1910 Schiele was immersed in the explorative portraiture with which he is most closely identified.

The bold graphic intensity Schiele brought to bear in his work during this period, along with his masterful use of line and vibrant color, began to bring him new stature as an artist. In 1913 and 1914 he participated in numerous exhibitions in a number of German cities, further enhancing his reputation. In March 1918 Schiele was given an entire room at the Vienna Secession, finally garnering recognition and financial success in his own city. But his enjoyment of his success was short-lived. In October 1918 he and his wife, Edith, died within four days of each other, victims of the Spanish flu epidemic ravaging Europe. Egon Schiele was twenty-eight.

Egon Schiele (Austrian, 1890–1918)

Seated Couple (Egon and Edith Schiele), 1915
Gouache and pencil on paper, 20⅝ x 16¼ in.
Courtesy Graphische Sammlung Albertina, Vienna

Pomegranate, Box 6099, Rohnert Park, CA 94927

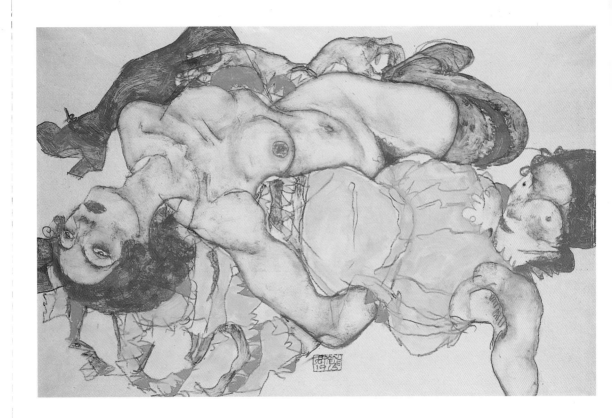

Egon Schiele (Austrian, 1890–1918)
Two Girls, Lying Entwined, 1915
Gouache and pencil on paper, 12⅞ x 19⅝ in.
Courtesy Graphische Sammlung Albertina, Vienna

Pomegranate, Box 6099, Rohnert Park, CA 94927

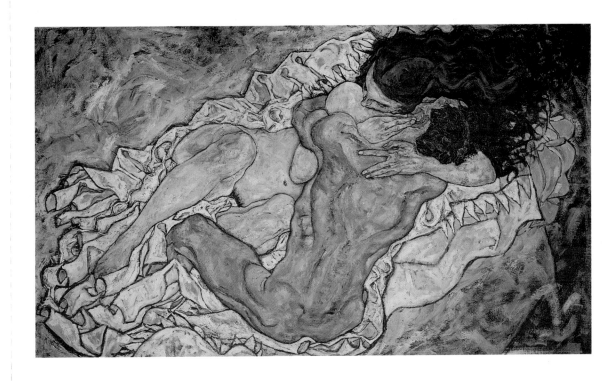

Egon Schiele (Austrian, 1890–1918)
Embrace (Lovers II), 1917
Oil on canvas, 39⅜ x 67 in.
Courtesy Archiv für Kunst und Geschichte, Berlin

Pomegranate, Box 6099, Rohnert Park, CA 94927

Egon Schiele (Austrian, 1890–1918)
The Family (Squatting Couple), 1918
Oil on canvas, 60 x 64 in.
Courtesy Archiv für Kunst und Geschichte, Berlin

Pomegranate, Box 6099, Rohnert Park, CA 94927

Egon Schiele (Austrian, 1890–1918)
Two Little Girls, 1911
Gouache, watercolor and pencil, 15¾ x 12 in.
Courtesy Graphische Sammlung Albertina, Vienna

Pomegranate, Box 6099, Rohnert Park, CA 94927

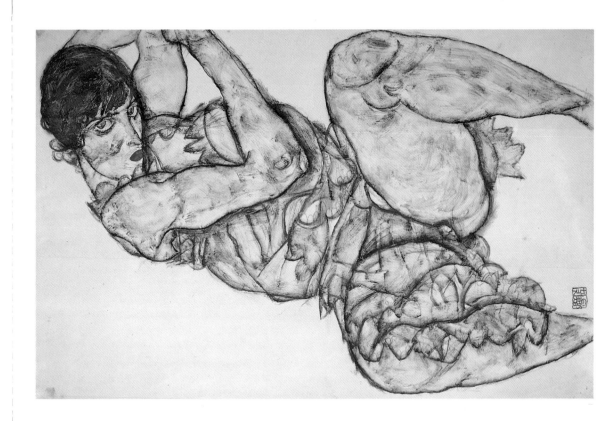

Egon Schiele (Austrian, 1890–1918)

Seated Woman with Left Hand in Hair, 1914
Gouache and pencil on paper, 19⅛ x 12⅜ in.
Courtesy Graphische Sammlung Albertina, Vienna

Pomegranate, Box 6099, Rohnert Park, CA 94927

Egon Schiele (Austrian, 1890–1918)

Nude on Her Stomach, 1917
Gouache and black crayon on paper, 11¾ x 18⅛ in.
Courtesy Graphische Sammlung Albertina, Vienna

Pomegranate, Box 6099, Rohnert Park, CA 94927

Egon Schiele (Austrian, 1890–1918)

Reclining Female Nude with Green Cap, Leaning to the Right,
1914
Watercolor and pencil on paper, 12⅝ x 19⅛ in.
Courtesy Graphische Sammlung Albertina, Vienna

Pomegranate, Box 6099, Rohnert Park, CA 94927

Egon Schiele (Austrian, 1890–1918)
Portrait of Gerti Schiele, 1909
Oil and metallic paint on canvas, 55⅜ x 55⅛ in.
Courtesy The Bridgeman Art Library, London

Pomegranate, Box 6099, Rohnert Park, CA 94927

Egon Schiele (Austrian, 1890–1918)
Cardinal and Nun (Caress), 1912
Oil on canvas, 27½ x 31½ in.
Courtesy Archiv für Kunst und Geschichte, Berlin

Pomegranate, Box 6099, Rohnert Park, CA 94927

Egon Schiele (Austrian, 1890–1918)
Self-Portrait with Chinese Lantern Plant, 1912
Oil and gouache on wood, 12¼ x 15¾ in.
Courtesy Archiv für Kunst und Geschichte, Berlin

Pomegranate, Box 6099, Rohnert Park, CA 94927

Egon Schiele (Austrian, 1890–1918)
Portrait of Valerie Neuzil, 1912
Oil on wood, 12⅝ x 15¾ in.
Courtesy Archiv für Kunst und Geschichte, Berlin

Pomegranate, Box 6099, Rohnert Park, CA 94927

Egon Schiele (Austrian, 1890–1918)
Self-Portrait with Hand to Cheek, 1910
Gouache, watercolor and charcoal on paper, 17½ x 12 in.
Courtesy Graphische Sammlung Albertina, Vienna

Pomegranate, Box 6099, Rohnert Park, CA 94927

Egon Schiele (Austrian, 1890–1918)
Two Girls Embracing (Two Friends), 1915
Gouache, watercolor and pencil on paper, 18⅞ x 12⅞ in.
Courtesy The Bridgeman Art Library, London

Pomegranate, Box 6099, Rohnert Park, CA 94927

Egon Schiele (Austrian, 1890–1918)

Crouching Male Nude (Self-Portrait), 1917
Gouache, watercolor and black crayon on paper, 18 x 11½ in.
Courtesy Graphische Sammlung Albertina, Vienna

Pomegranate, Box 6099, Rohnert Park, CA 94927

Egon Schiele (Austrian, 1890–1918)

The Hermits, 1912
Oil on canvas, 71¼ x 71¼ in.
Courtesy Archiv für Kunst und Geschichte, Berlin

Pomegranate, Box 6099, Rohnert Park, CA 94927

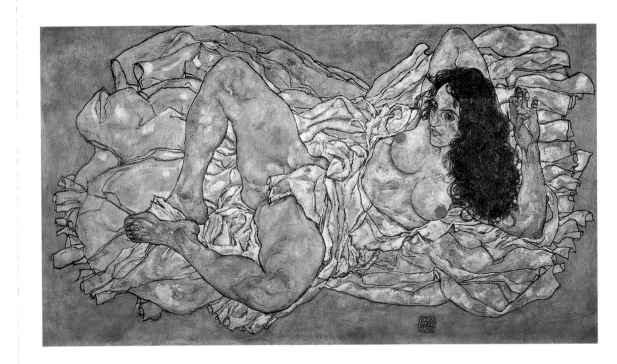

Egon Schiele (Austrian, 1890–1918)
Reclining Woman, 1917
Oil on canvas, 37$\frac{25}{32}$ x 67$\frac{5}{16}$ in.
Courtesy Archiv für Kunst und Geschichte, Berlin

Pomegranate, Box 6099, Rohnert Park, CA 94927

Egon Schiele (Austrian, 1890–1918)
Portrait of the Painter Hans Massmann, 1909
Oil and metallic paint on canvas, 47¼ x 43¼ in.
Private collection

Pomegranate, Box 6099, Rohnert Park, CA 94927

Egon Schiele (Austrian, 1890–1918)
The Painter Max Oppenheimer, Three-Quarter Length, 1910
Watercolor, ink and black crayon on paper, 17¾ x 11¾ in.
Courtesy Graphische Sammlung Albertina, Vienna

Pomegranate, Box 6099, Rohnert Park, CA 94927

Egon Schiele (Austrian, 1890–1918)
Blind Mother, 1914
Oil on canvas, 39⅛ x 47⅜ in.
Courtesy Archiv für Kunst und Geschichte, Berlin

Pomegranate, Box 6099, Rohnert Park, CA 94927

Egon Schiele (Austrian, 1890–1918)
Mother with Two Children III, 1917
Oil on canvas, 59 x 62½ in.
Courtesy The Bridgeman Art Library, London

Pomegranate, Box 6099, Rohnert Park, CA 94927

Egon Schiele (Austrian, 1890–1918)
Portrait of the Artist's Sister Gerti, 1910
Watercolor and black crayon on paper with white
heightening
Number 288 in a series of postcards published by the Wiener
Werkstätte (Vienna Workshop), 1907–1914
From the collection of Der Salzburger Landessammlungen
Rupertinum, Austria

Pomegranate, Box 6099, Rohnert Park, CA 94927

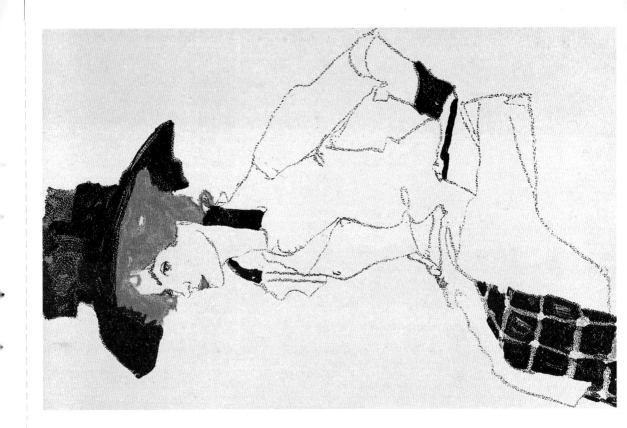

Egon Schiele (Austrian, 1890–1918)
Portrait of Woman with Big Hat (Gertrude Schiele), 1910
Watercolor and black crayon on paper
Number 289 in a series of postcards published by the Wiener
Werkstätte (Vienna Workshop), 1907–1914
From the collection of Der Salzburger Landessammlungen
Rupertinum, Austria

Pomegranate, Box 6099, Rohnert Park, CA 94927

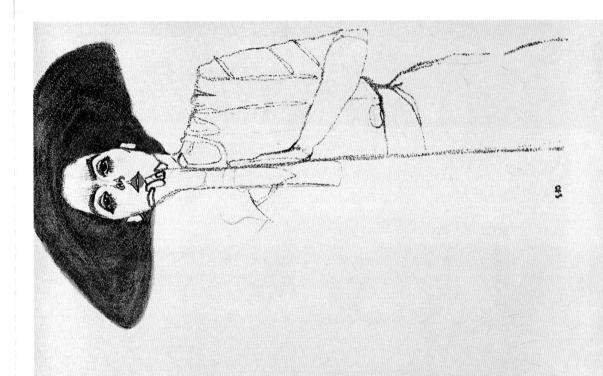

Egon Schiele (Austrian, 1890–1918)
Portrait of a Woman, 1910
Watercolor and black crayon on paper
Number 290 in a series of postcards published by the Wiener
Werkstätte (Vienna Workshop), 1907–1914
From the collection of Der Salzburger Landessammlungen
Rupertinum, Austria

Pomegranate, Box 6099, Rohnert Park, CA 94927

Egon Schiele (Austrian, 1890–1918)
Krumau Landscape (Town and River), 1916
Oil on canvas, 43½ x 55½ in.

Pomegranate, Box 6099, Rohnert Park, CA 94927

Egon Schiele (Austrian, 1890–1918)
Black-Haired Nude Girl, Standing, 1910
Watercolor and pencil on paper with white heightening,
21⅜ x 12⅛ in.
Courtesy Graphische Sammlung Albertina, Vienna

Pomegranate, Box 6099, Rohnert Park, CA 94927

Egon Schiele (Austrian, 1890–1918)

Schiele, Drawing a Nude Model Before a Mirror, 1910
Pencil on paper, 21¾ x 13⅞ in.
Courtesy Graphische Sammlung Albertina, Vienna

Pomegranate, Box 6099, Rohnert Park, CA 94927

Egon Schiele (Austrian, 1890–1918)
Sunflowers, 1911
Watercolor and pencil on paper, 19 x 12½ in.
Courtesy Graphische Sammlung Albertina, Vienna

Pomegranate, Box 6099, Rohnert Park, CA 94927

Egon Schiele (Austrian, 1890–1918)
Reclining Nude with Green Stockings, 1914
Gouache and pencil on paper, 12 x 18 in.
Private collection
Courtesy The Bridgeman Art Library, London

Pomegranate, Box 6099, Rohnert Park, CA 94927

Egon Schiele (Austrian, 1890–1918)
The Artist's Mother (Marie Schiele), 1918
Black crayon on paper, 16⅞ x 10½ in.
Courtesy Graphische Sammlung Albertina, Vienna

Pomegranate, Box 6099, Rohnert Park, CA 94927